910.92   Fradin, Dennis B.
FRA
         Explorers

$13.27

DATE		

A New True Book

EXPLORERS

By Dennis B. Fradin

CHILDRENS PRESS ™

CHICAGO

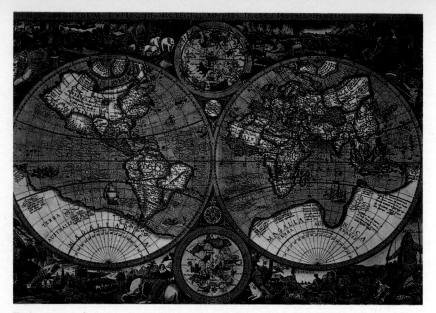

This map of the world, drawn by Pieter van den Keere in
1607, was based on a map drawn in 1594.

PHOTO CREDITS
Historical Pictures Service, Chicago—9 (2 photos), 14, 17 (left), 21, 32 (right), 35 (left)
The Granger Collection—2, 4 (3 photos), 7, 13, 17 (right), 19 (left), 25, 26, 28 (left), 30, 32 (left), 33 (2 photos), 34 (left), 35 (right), 44
Brown Brothers—10, 19 (right), 23 (left), 28 (right), 36
Emilie Lepthien—23 (right)
The Bettmann Archive—34 (right), 37 (2 photos), 39
Finley Holiday Film Corporation—41
DAVA, Still Media Depository, Washington, D.C.—42
Montana Historical Society—Cover
Cover: E.S. Paxson, "Lewis and Clark at Three Forks"

Library of Congress Cataloging in Publication Data

Fradin, Dennis B.
   Explorers.

   (A New true book)
   Includes index.
   Summary: Discusses the reasons people go exploring,
and traces the history of exploration from ancient
civilization through the space program.
   1. Explorers—Juvenile literature. [1. Explorers]
I. Title.
G175.F7   1984   910'.92'2   84-7077
ISBN 0-516-01926-0   AACR2

TABLE OF CONTENTS

Why Do People Explore?... 5

Early Explorations... 8

The Age of Discovery... 12

The Native People... 27

Explorations in Recent
  Centuries... 31

Exploring Other Worlds... 38

The Future of Exploration... 43

Words You Should Know... 46

Index... 47

Sculpture (above left) of Alexander the Great (356-323 B.C.). The thirteenth-century colored woodcut (above right) shows Alexander the Great exploring the ocean floor in a glass barrel. People often fear the unknown. This 1550 woodcut (below) shows the sea monsters and strange animals thought to live in the unexplored parts of the North Atlantic Ocean.

WHY DO PEOPLE EXPLORE ?

People who go to unknown lands are called explorers. From earliest times, human beings have explored new lands.

The earliest explorers discovered new lands in their search for food.

Conquerors, such as Alexander the Great, explored while making their empires bigger. Conquered people explored new places while looking for new homes.

Gold and other treasures have lured many explorers. The desire to spread religion has inspired many others. Still others wanted to trade for goods they did not have.

People have always wondered about distant

An engraving, made in 1592 by Theodor de Bry, shows ship leaving Lisbon, Portugal for a voyage of exploration to the New World.

places. Curiosity has caused people to sail across oceans, to rocket to the moon, and to dive beneath the seas.

EARLY EXPLORATIONS

Hennu, an Egyptian, was the first explorer whose name we know. More than four thousand years ago Hennu led a sea voyage to the Land of Punt, which was somewhere in Africa. Hennu and other Egyptian explorers were searching for gold, ivory, and cinnamon.

Several thousand years ago the Phoenicians (who

Old drawings show Hennu fighting a gorilla in Africa (left) and the ships (above) Hennu used to sail to the Land of Punt.

lived in what are now Syria, Lebanon, and Israel) explored the Mediterranean Sea and the Atlantic Ocean. The Carthaginians (who lived in northern Africa) explored parts of

9

Alexander the Great won victories in India. Here he accepts the surrender of the Indian Rajah Porus about 326 B.C.

Africa. The Greeks explored much of Europe and Asia as they conquered.

One fact became clear—the world was much bigger than most people

had thought. Greek
scientists tried to figure its
size. One of them,
Eratosthenes, said that the
distance around the earth
was 25,000 miles at the
equator. He was almost
exactly right. Eratosthenes,
Pythagoras, and other
Greek scientists also
claimed that the world was
round.

Many people laughed at
this idea. They believed
the earth was flat.

THE AGE OF DISCOVERY

About A.D. 982, a
Norwegian, Eric the Red,
explored Greenland. About
A.D. 1000, Leif Ericsson,
son of Eric the Red, sailed
west from Greenland to a
place he named Vinland.
Vinland was probably in
Canada.

Despite these voyages,
few important explorations
were made until the late
1400s. Then things

Painting showing Leif Ericsson's discovery of America

changed. In fact, so many
explorations were made
from the late 1400s
through the 1500s that this
time is called the Age of
Discovery.

One of the first great voyages was made by the Portuguese Bartolomeu Dias. In 1487 and 1488 Dias sailed around the Cape of Good Hope near Africa's southern tip. This discovery was important.

Bartolomeu Dias was the first to sail around the Cape of Good Hope.

Now ships from Europe could sail east to Asia. Their captains could trade for spices and other goods.

Another explorer, Christopher Columbus, thought the best way to get to Asia from Europe was to sail west. In August of 1492 Columbus sailed west from Spain with three ships—the *Nina,* the *Pinta,* and the *Santa Maria.*

The ships traveled about one hundred miles per day. As the sailors went farther and farther out into the Atlantic Ocean they wondered if they would ever see land again.

At 2:00 in the morning of October 12, 1492, the lookout on the *Pinta* yelled, *"Tierra, tierra!"* ("Land, land!").

Columbus thought he had reached one of the islands of the Indies, near

The caravels of Christopher Columbus (left), and a nineteenth-century engraving showing Columbus landing at San Salvador in the Bahamas on October 12, 1492 (right).

China. Because of this, he named the people he met Indians. Actually Columbus had arrived at San Salvador, an island in the Bahamas.

Today Columbus is often called the discoverer of America. But Leif Ericsson had been to America nearly five hundred years earlier. And Indians had explored America twenty thousand years before Ericsson! It is more accurate to say that Columbus was the first modern explorer to reach the Americas.

Columbus made three more voyages to the Americas. On January 2,

1525 portrait of Christopher Columbus (left). Reconstruction of the *Santa Maria* (right).

1494, during his second trip, he founded the settlement of Isabela on the island of Hispaniola. This was the first European settlement in the Americas. Later Columbus explored parts of Central and South

America and some islands
in the Caribbean Sea.

In 1519, Ferdinand
Magellan made what is
often called the world's
most important exploration.

On September 20, 1519,
Magellan sailed from
Spain. His five ships carried
250 men. Magellan had
been hired by Spain to sail
west to the Spice Islands
(also called the Moluccas)
in Indonesia to buy spices.

After sailing around
South America's southern

Ferdinand Magellan's fleet sailed around the southern tip of South America and into the Pacific Ocean.

tip, Magellan reached an ocean that he named the Pacific, meaning "peaceful." He couldn't know how vast was this new ocean. For two months he and his men didn't see land. After running out of food they had to eat sawdust and rats and drink dirty water. As the days went by, more and more men died.

Finally Magellan and his crew spotted an island that they named Saint Paul's Island. There the crew caught seabirds and fish. When a storm struck they drank rainwater.

After leaving Saint Paul's, the sailors stopped at Guam and other Pacific

Magellan (left) planted a cross in the Philippine Islands. Today Magellan's cross is in a shrine in the city of Cebu, on the Philippine Islands.

islands for food and fresh water. Unfortunately, Magellan became involved in a battle between two tribes in the Philippines and was killed.

Soon only two of the five ships remained. After reaching the Spice Islands the two took on a cargo of cloves. One of the ships tried to return to Spain the way it had come. It didn't make it. The last ship, the *Victoria,* sailed westward. Its captain, Juan Sebastian del Cano, sailed the *Victoria* back to Spain. On September 6, 1522, the *Victoria* became the first

Magellan's ship, *Victoria,* was pictured on this 1590 map
of the Pacific Ocean drawn by Abraham Ortelius.

ship to have sailed around
the world!

Only eighteen men had
lived through the three-year

1695 woodcut
of Ferdinand
Magellan

voyage. They had proved that the world is round. Although Ferdinand Magellan hadn't survived the voyage, he is often called the greatest sailor who ever lived.

THE NATIVE PEOPLE

When explorers found new lands, they also found people already living in these lands. Explorers often abused these natives.

Christopher Columbus captured and enslaved Indians. In the 1530s the

Francisco Pizarro (left) explored South America. He and his men killed thousands of Inca Indians (right) in Peru.

Spaniard Francisco Pizarro
and his men killed
thousands of Inca Indians
in South America and
destroyed their culture. In

28

Africa, millions of black Africans were sold into slavery.

Even when explorers didn't mistreat natives, the people who came later often did. The natives' land, treasures, and even their freedom were often taken from them. Is it surprising that the natives sometimes attacked the outsiders?

Henry Hudson explored the Hudson River in the *Half Moon*.

EXPLORATIONS
IN RECENT CENTURIES

Despite all the voyages during the Age of Discovery, the earth still had unexplored regions. During the 1600s many explorers came to North America.

Henry Hudson discovered Canada's Hudson Bay and

Because of Henry Hudson's (above) explorations, England claimed much of what is now eastern Canada.

explored the Hudson River in what is now the United States.

In 1769 Englishman James Cook became the first European to set foot on New Zealand. In 1778 he became the first

James Cook (left) explored the Hawaiian Islands (above) and much of the South Pacific during the 1760s and 1770s.

European known to reach the Hawaiian Islands.

During the 1800s there were many African explorers. In 1851 the Scotsman David Livingstone explored the Zambezi River. In 1855 he

Sir Henry Morton Stanley (left), a journalist and explorer, and David Livingstone (right), a missionary, both explored the African interior.

discovered Victoria Falls. In 1877 the Welshman Sir Henry Morton Stanley explored the Congo River. Englishwoman Mary Kingsley, in 1895, became

Stanley on the shores of Lake
Tanganyika (left). Engraving of the historic meeting
of Stanley and Livingstone on November 10, 1871
at Ujiji, Lake Tanganyika (above).

the first European to visit
several places in western
Africa.

As the 1900s began,
there were still two big
challenges for explorers—
the North and South Poles.

Robert E. Peary

Between 1800 and 1908 there had been more than five hundred attempts to reach the North Pole. In 1908 the American Robert E. Peary set out on his third try. On April 6, 1909,

Captain Roald Amundsen (right) led an expedition to the South
Pole. Using a sextant and artificial horizon, Amundsen
proved he was the first explorer to reach the South Pole.

Peary reached the North
Pole. In December of 1911
the Norwegian explorer
Roald Amundsen made it
to the South Pole.

EXPLORING OTHER WORLDS

In the 1950s a new age of exploration began—the space age. It started on October 4, 1957, when Russia launched the satellite *Sputnik I.*

After this, Russia and the United States launched other satellites and sent people into space.

On the morning of July 16, 1969, astronauts Neil

From left to right: Astronauts Edwin E. Aldrin, Jr., lunar pilot, Michael Collins, command module pilot, and Neil A. Armstrong, commander

A. Armstrong, Edwin Aldrin, Jr., and Michael Collins blasted off in their *Apollo 11* rocket.

At 10:56 P.M. on July 20, 1969, as millions of people watched on TV, Armstrong left the ship and became the first person to walk on the moon.

Between 1969 and 1972 six moon landings were made. Each team explored a different part of the moon.

Apollo 15 astronaut, James B. Irwin salutes the flag. The lunar lander, *Falcon,* and the lunar rover, the car the astronauts used to explore the moon, are also shown.

Voyager spacecraft explored Jupiter and other planets.

In recent years, unmanned space probes have been launched to photograph and study other planets. Using probes, scientists can explore distant worlds without risking human lives.

The *Sealab III Habitat* (above) and the bathyscaphe
Trieste I (below) are used to explore the ocean.

THE FUTURE
OF EXPLORATION

Earth still has unexplored places. The oceans, which cover 70 percent of our planet's surface, still hold many secrets. But the most exciting future explorations will be made on other worlds.

One day explorers will travel to the planets. Brave,

Engraving showing Hernando de Soto's discovery of the Mississippi River in 1541.

intelligent people will be needed for such voyages — people like Ferdinand Magellan, Christopher Columbus, and Mary Kingsley. Would you like to make such an exploration?

SOME FAMOUS EXPLORERS

Explorer	Nationality	Exploration	Date
Hennu	Egyptian	Land of Punt, on coast of Red Sea	About 2000 B.C.
Hanno	Carthaginian	Northwest coast of Africa	About 500 B.C.
Alexander the Great	Greek	India	327 B.C.
Eric the Red	Norwegian	Greenland	About A.D. 982
Leif Ericsson	Norwegian	Vinland, which was probably in eastern Canada	About A.D. 1000
Marco Polo	Italian	China and other areas in Asia	1271-1295
Bartolomeu Dias	Portuguese	Rounded Cape of Good Hope	1487-1488
Christopher Columbus	Italian	America (San Salvador Island, in the Bahamas)	1492
Vasco da Gama	Portuguese	Led first sea voyage to India from Europe	1498
Juan Ponce de León	Spanish	Florida	1513
Vasco Núñez de Balboa	Spanish	Sighted Pacific Ocean	1513
Ferdinand Magellan	Portuguese	Commander of first voyage around world	1519-1521
Juan Sebastián del Cano	Spanish	Completed Magellan's voyage	1519-1522
Francisco Pizarro	Spanish	Peru, where he founded Lima	1531-1535
Hernando de Soto	Spanish	Mississippi River and southeastern United States	1539-1542
Henry Hudson	English	Hudson River, Hudson Strait, and Hudson Bay in North America	1609-1611
Sieur de La Salle	French	Lake Michigan area and Mississippi River	1679-1682
James Cook	English	First European known to reach Hawaiian Islands	1778
Meriwether Lewis and William Clark	American	Traveled across Rocky Mountains to Pacific Ocean and back	1804-1806
David Livingstone	Scottish	Zambezi River, Victoria Falls, and other places in Africa	1849-1873
Sir Henry Morton Stanley	Welsh	Congo River and several other places in Africa	1874-1889
Robert E. Peary	American	Leader of first expedition to arrive at North Pole	1909
Roald Amundsen	Norwegian	First person to arrive at South Pole	1911
Neil A. Armstrong	American	First person to walk on moon	1969

WORDS YOU SHOULD KNOW

astronauts(AST • roh • nawts) — space explorers

caravel(kair • ah • VEL) — a strong sailing ship, developed in the 1400s, which could make long voyages

civilization(siv • ih • lih • ZAY • shun) — a society with a fairly advanced way of life

coast(COH • st) — the land along a large body of water

commander(kuh • MAN • der) — leader

compass(KUM • pess) — a device used to determine directions

conquerors(KONG • ker • rerz)people who have defeated other people

culture(KUL • cher) — a people's way of life

curious(KYOOR • ee • us) — interested in learning

discovery(dis • KUV • ree) — the act of finding out about something before anyone else

equator(eh • KWAY • ter) — an imaginary circle around the earth, halfway between the North Pole and South Pole

exploration(ex • plor • RAY • shun) — the process of exploring

explorer(ex • PLOR • er) — a person who visits and studies unknown lands

intelligent(in • TEL • ih • gent) — having a good mind

natives(NAY • tivz) — people who have made a particular place their home for some time

orbit(OR • bit) — the path an object takes when it moves around another object

prehistoric(pre • hiss • TORE • ick) — belonging to the time before written history

settlers(SET • lerz) — people who have recently moved into an area

space probes(SPAISS PROHBZ) — devices that send back information from outer space

spices(SPY • sez) — vegetable products, such as pepper, used to flavor foods

unexplored(un • ex • PLORD) — not yet explored

valuable(VAL • yoo • uh • bil) — having great worth

voyage(VOI • ij) — a trip

INDEX

Africa, 8, 9, 10, 14, 29, 33-35
Age of Discovery, 13, 31
Aldrin, Edwin, Jr., 39
Alexander the Great, 5
Americas, 18, 19
Amundsen, Roald, 37
Apollo 11 rocket, 39
Armstrong, Neil A., 38-39
Asia, 10, 15
Atlantic Ocean, 9, 16
Bahamas, 17
Canada, 12, 31
Cano, Juan Sebastián del, 24
Caribbean Sea, 20
Carthaginians, 9
Central America, 19-20
chart: famous explorers, 45
China, 17
cinnamon, 8
Collins, Michael, 39
Columbus, Christopher, 15-19, 27, 44
Congo River, 34
Cook, James, 32
curiosity, 7
Dias, Bartolomeu, 14,
earth, size of, 10, 11
Egypt, 8
Eratosthenes, 11
Eric the Red, 12

Europe, 10, 15
food, 5
gold, 6, 8
Greeks, 10, 11
Greenland, 12
Guam, 22
Hawaiian Islands, 33
Hennu, 8
Hispaniola, 19
Hudson, Henry, 31
Hudson Bay, 31
Hudson River, 32
Inca Indians, 28
Indians, 17, 18, 27, 28
Indies, 16
Indonesia, 20
Isabela, 19
Israel, 9
ivory, 8
Kingsley, Mary, 34, 44
Lebanon, 9
Leif Ericsson, 12, 18
Livingstone, David, 33
Magellan, Ferdinand, 20-23, 26, 44
Mediterranean Sea, 9
Moluccas (Spice Islands), 20, 24
moon walk, 40
New Zealand, 32
Nina (ship), 15

North America, 31
North Pole, 35-37
Norway, 12, 37
oceans, unexplored, 43
Pacific Ocean, 21, 22
Peary, Robert E., 36, 37
Philippines, 23
Phoenicians, 8
Pinta (ship), 15, 16
Pizarro, Francisco, 28
planets, exploration of, 41, 43
Punt, Land of, 8
Pythagoras, 11
religion, 6
Russia, 38
Saint Paul's Island, 22
San Salvador, 17

Santa Maria (ship), 15
slavery, 29
South America, 19-20, 28
South Pole, 35, 37
space exploration, 38-41
Spain, 15, 20, 24
Spice Islands (Moluccas), 20, 24
Sputnik I, 38
Stanley, Sir Henry Morton, 34
Syria, 9
trade, 6, 15
United States, 32, 38
Victoria (ship), 24
Victoria Falls, 34
Vinland, 12
Zambezi River, 33

About the Author

Dennis Fradin attended Northwestern University on a partial creative writing scholarship and was graduated in 1967. He has published stories and articles in such places as Ingenue, The Saturday Evening Post, Scholastic, Chicago, Oui, *and* National Humane Review. *His previous books include the Young People's Stories of Our States series for Childrens Press, and* Bad Luck Tony *for Prentice-Hall. In the True book series Dennis has written about astronomy, farming, comets, archaeology, movies, and the space lab. He is married and the father of three children.*